The *D*iscipleship *S*eries

Other titles in the series

8
Ways to
Deepen
Your Faith

Published by CWR, Waverley Abbey House,
Waverley Lane, Farnham, Surrey GU9 8EP, England.

Front cover image: Helen Reason.
Illustrations: Helen Reason.

Unless otherwise indicated, all Scripture references are from the Holy Bible:
New International Version (NIV), copyright a 1973, 1978, 1984 by the
International Bible Society

Other Scripture quotations are marked:
Amplified: *The Amplified Bible*, a 1987, Zondervan Corporation and the
Lockman Foundation
AV: *The Authorised Version*
Moffatt: *The Moffatt Translation of the Bible*, a 1987, Hodder & Stoughton
NASB: *New American Standard Bible*, a 1977, Lockman Corporation
NKJ: *New King James Version*, a 1982, Thomas Nelson Inc.
Phillips: J.B. Phillips, *The New Testament in Modern English*, a 1960, 1972,
Fount Paperbacks
RSV: *Revised Standard Version*, a 1965, Division of Christian Education of the National
Council of the Churches of Christ in the United States of America
TLB: *The Living Bible*, a 1971, 1994, Tyndale House Publishers

ISBN 1 85345 215 7

Concept development, editing, design and production by CWR.

Typesetting: David Andrew Design.
Printed by Omnia Books Ltd.

8
Ways to Deepen Your Faith

Selwyn Hughes

Contents

Introduction

"The apostles said to the Lord, 'Increase our faith!' " (Luke 17:5)

I once read about a church in New York which is situated next door to a beauty salon. The beauty salon put up a sign saying, "Come inside and have your *face* lifted." The church went one better and put up a sign that read, "Come inside and have your *faith* lifted."

The theme of this book, ways to deepen our faith, came to me when, some years ago, in a prayer meeting, the Spirit whispered these words to me: "*My people are being destroyed.*" When I asked why, the Spirit seemed to say, "Because of their lack of faith." These words crystallised a conviction within me that one of the most urgent needs in the life of the Christian Church today is for God's people to possess and demonstrate a stronger and more vibrant faith. Many believers – the number is appalling – are living their lives on a level far below what God intends.

They lack faith – and therefore lack power. The age in which we are living is increasing in evil, and if we Christians are to meet the challenge of this hour, there must be a corresponding increase in our faith. So, let me ask you, right at the beginning of this book, a pointed and personal question. How vigorous and vibrant is your faith? Is it just something you hold – or is it something that holds you?

Think back to the story about the signs outside the beauty salon and the church. Perhaps you are already aware that your faith needs lifting, perhaps that's why you have started to read this book. There are times when we all need to be lifted.   But take a look at the verse from Luke's Gospel at the top of the previous page – what is it that Jesus' disciples ask for? Not simply for a lifting of faith but an *enlarging*. Make their prayer your own, personalise it so that it reads not "Increase our faith", but "Increase my faith". Do it now.

1

Living
by **faith**

"... the just shall live by his faith." (Habakkuk 2:4, AV)

How vital and important is this matter of faith in Christian life and experience? Do we regard it as something merely desirable – or something indispensable?

The verse with which we begin this chapter shows quite clearly that in relation to the life lived before God, faith is not something that is optional, but something that is obligatory. It is not a matter of personal preference; it is a definite priority.

Dr G. Campbell Morgan, the well-known Bible expositor, described the statement, "the just shall live by faith", as "the mightiest sentence in the Book of God". Another commentator says that this verse is "the hinge on which the doors of Scripture are opened". Yet another says, "Apart from John 3:16 – it is the greatest word ever."

Why should this statement be regarded so highly by Bible expositors? Because it condenses into a single phrase a truth that is found everywhere from Genesis to Revelation – *the life which pleases God is the life of faith.*

Many Christians regard faith as a special quality which they hold in reserve to deal with difficult or perplexing situations, and while to some extent this might be true, faith in its primary sense is the underlying principle which governs all Christian living – from start to finish.

Faith is far more than a channel through which we receive special favours; it is a calling, a daily walk. It is not just a force in Christian living – it is the focus of it. Not just an optional extra, but an everyday necessity. The issue, then, is inescapable – we live by faith, or we do not live at all.

A prophet in confusion

Habakkuk was bewildered. He begins his prophecy in the midst of utter confusion: "O Lord, how long must I call for help before you will listen?" (Hab. 1:2, TLB). The prophet was confused and frustrated by the continuance of evil. He could not understand why God did not intervene to restrain injustice within Judah or the evil nations around him and he was frustrated by God's apparent slowness in dealing with this issue.

After expressing his feelings, Habakkuk decides to give up the task of trying to reason things out and instead takes a leap of faith. He says, in effect, "I will go up to my watchtower and wait for God." Those who are willing to *wait* for God to speak are never disappointed. Notice Habakkuk's words: "*Then* the Lord replied" (2:2). When? Then – after Habakkuk had indicated his willingness to wait.

The vision came in the form of words: "The just shall live by his faith" (AV), which Habakkuk was told to clearly inscribe on tablets for the heralds to run with, not so that he who reads may run, but that he who runs may read (Hab. 2:2). In other words, it is a message for even the busiest of people.

Those who tear through life, never pausing for prayerful thought and consideration, must get hold of this or else they are at the mercy of every wind and circumstance. Are you rushing through life trying to resolve the world's problems? Then stop and get hold of this: *the just shall live by faith.*

God knows what He is doing – so just trust Him. Hold on to that, and never again will your feet slip and slide on the rocky slopes of life. You will have, as did Habakkuk, "hinds' feet ... on my high places" (3:19, NASB).

Immediately preceding the famous statement on faith come these words – "Behold, as for the proud one, his soul is not right within him" (Hab. 2:4, NASB). Unfortunately these words tend to be overshadowed by the sublime statement, "the just shall live by his faith", and are seldom quoted – but in fact they are extremely important. In this verse God is showing us that there are only two possible attitudes to life – faith or unbelief.

Our outlook is either based on belief in Him or denial of Him, and these two philosophies of life are diametrically opposed. The first is that of the proud. Some translations use the words "swollen" or "puffed up", a graphic picture of pride and self-sufficiency. That is one philosophy of life – proud, puffed up, swollen, self-sufficient. The other philosophy is that of the just – those who have a sense of certainty in spite of adverse circumstances, and who walk through life with confidence and poise.

This is what Dr Martyn Lloyd-Jones described as "the 'great watershed of life' – and all of us are on one side of it or the other". Life, when stripped to its irreducible minimum, consists of one of two attitudes: *we take what God says and live by it, or else we do not.* This is the lesson Habakkuk learned as he sat in his watchtower, and it is one that we must learn before we move any further.

Facet by facet

God's answer to a perplexed and confused prophet – the just shall live by faith – was, and is, the revelation of the basic principle of human life. Either we live by faith, or we do not live at all. The phrase is found not only in the prophecy of Habakkuk, but is repeated on three separate occasions in the New Testament – each one having immense and deep significance.

It is as if God plucks this jewel out of the Old Testament and holds it up in the New, slowly turning it facet by facet, so that we can take in even more of its truth and beauty.

The first time it appears is in the book of Romans chapter 1 verse 17. Why Romans? Well, Romans is the letter in which Paul deals with the great truths of salvation, showing how God has accomplished the task of *justifying* sinners. The emphasis in Romans is therefore on the word "just": the *just* shall live by faith. What a wonderful thing it is to be "justified by faith". It means, quite simply, that those who believe and accept the fact of Christ's substitutionary death on Calvary stand in God's presence *just as if* they had never sinned.

A bank manager's little son was standing by his father's desk. Where he stood, a shaft of sunlight was shining directly on him, and he said, "Daddy, I'm standing in the smile of God." The father replied wistfully, "I wish I could stand in the smile of God." We all wish just that! The good news of the gospel is that when we stand in Christ, we stand in God's smile. Some feel they are standing in God's frown, but all they have to do is to move over into His smile. That's justification.

The second time the statement appears in the New Testament is in the book of Galatians: "... no man is justified by the law in the sight of God ... for, The just shall live by faith" (Gal. 3.11, AV). Galatians is supremely the letter of *freedom*. Here Paul proclaims the truth that, in Christ, the Christian is set free from every yoke of bondage which can be placed upon the human soul. There were those in the Galatian churches who felt that Christ was not enough. They wanted "Christ and" – in this case, Christ and circumcision. Without the "and" their salvation was not complete.

How sad that in the twenty-first-century Church we try to do the same: Christ *and* becoming a member of our church; Christ *and* our interpretation of Him; Christ *and* our doctrinal slogans; Christ *and* our forms of worship. Endlessly we say "Christ *and*". Paul refused to add any "and" to Christ. The freedom he portrayed in Christ was a freedom from endless "ands". Christ and Christ alone is necessary to salvation.

Judaism, it is said, contained 3,600 laws which had to be obeyed. What a relief to learn that in Christ they are reduced to two – love God, and love your neighbour as yourself. If we keep these, then all the others are kept – automatically. What a way to live! We are freed from complexity to simplicity, from the marginal to the central, from the trivial to the great. "The just shall *live* by faith."

The third and last occasion where the words "the just shall live by faith" are found in the New Testament is in Hebrews 10:38. This letter is pre-eminently the epistle of faith, and it reveals how living by this principle enables us to triumph over all kinds of difficulties and problems. Unquestionably the purpose of the author was to establish and strengthen the early Hebrew Christians who felt that they had lost so much, having turned from the grand ritual and ceremony of the Hebrew religion to the simpler but more effective things of Christ.

If Romans places the emphasis on the word *just*, and Galatians on the word *live*, then Hebrews places it on the word *faith*. Romans emphasises the fact that faith enables us to stand in the sight of God *just as if* we had never sinned. Galatians draws our attention to the truth that, in Christ, we are freed from endless bondages. In Him we *live* – and how!

Paul himself was an example of the truth which he taught to the Galatians: "I live by faith in the Son of God, who loved me and gave himself for me" (Gal. 2:20). Hebrews makes the point that we considered earlier, namely, that faith is the underlying principle which governs all Christian living – from start to finish.

The life that the just person shall live is a life of *faith*. One famous missionary put it like this: "Every moment of the day – not just on certain specific occasions – a Christian has to exercise faith. We *live* by it. Indeed the Christian life would be paralysed without it." This being true, then why do not more of us lay a greater hold on faith and live by it?

2

Discovering
what **faith** is not

"... if you confess with your mouth, 'Jesus is Lord,' and believe in your heart ... you will be saved." (Romans 10:9)

What precisely is faith? What is its nature and what are its constituent parts? I am compelled to say right away that, in my experience, the subject of faith tends to cause more confusion and misunderstanding than any other in the Bible.

Great confusion exists even over the meaning of the word. One woman, when asked how she became a member of a church, said, "I joined it on 'confusion of faith'." She meant, of course, "*confession* of faith".

Some see faith as a magic lamp which they rub, and hey presto – all their wishes come true. Others see it, as we said before, as something that functions in their lives only on certain occasions. I think it might be helpful if, before arriving at a definition of what faith is, we consider *what it is not*. In this way we might be better able to understand the definition when we come to it.

1. Faith is not mere intellectual acceptance

A person can have an intellectual belief in everything the Church and the Bible affirm, and not have faith. One of the great tragedies of today is that people sit in church, Sunday after Sunday, reciting creeds and yet having no real contact with the Creator. Now I am not against creeds – indeed, whenever we formulate a statement of faith, we have a creed. In a sense every Christian, though he may not recite it, subscribes to a creed. Faith is not merely the acceptance of certain truths *about* God; faith goes beyond those truths to touch God Himself. It is launching out on the biggest hypothesis one knows – God – not with one's lips, but with one's life.

2. Faith is not blind credulity

I have referred before to the story of the boy who, when asked to define faith, said, "Faith is believing something you know isn't true." That is not faith; that is credulity.

Some Christians so want to possess faith that they believe, not in the impossible, but in the ridiculous. A man I knew in a church in Wales once said to me, "I am praying for God to give me £10,000 for a certain project I want to embark upon for Him." "And how do you expect God to answer that request?" I asked. He said, "I believe He will create 10,000 new banknotes and make them appear in my desk drawer."

Now I would be the last person in the world to dampen or destroy anyone's faith, but quite frankly, I thought his request was ridiculous – and I told him so. How could God create brand new banknotes without upsetting the numerical sequence of those already in circulation? He could, of course, create banknotes with different numbers from those already in print, but imagine what consternation that would cause in banking circles. They would be regarded, quite rightly, as false and fraudulent.

God is able and willing to do the impossible, but He is not

willing to do the unreasonable. John Stott says that faith is a *reasoning* trust. Notice that: not just trust, but a *reasoning* trust. And why? Because faith rests on the character of God, and since God is reasonable – then faith must be reasonable also.

Not naïve

3. Faith is not naïve optimism

The right type of optimism, of course, can be a very desirable quality, and it is undoubtedly true that optimism, in its purest form, is an ingredient of faith. There are many Christians, however, whose use of optimism is incredibly naïve – to say the least. I once saw a church poster that said, "Cheer up – it may never happen!" Imagine someone who had suffered a tragic loss, such as a bereavement or a financial catastrophe, reading that! It was so naïve that it was absurd.

The best illustration I know of *naïve* optimism is the story of a man who, having fallen from the top floor of a twenty-storey building was heard to say, as he passed the eleventh floor – "So far, so good!"

A teaching that is quietly spreading in some Christian communities says that it is the nature of faith to ignore reality and focus only on the finality. It sounds plausible, but it's not true. Faith never ignores reality. Naïve optimism may do that, but faith – never!

The attitude of mind that will not look difficulties in the face and admit they are there is deeply suspect. It is not a healthy thing to do – either mentally or spiritually. That does not mean we should go to the other extreme and focus our gaze solely upon our problems – for if we look too long at them, we will be adversely affected by them.

We must look at our problems, but we must not focus on them. We glance at them, but we gaze at God. True faith looks difficulties in the face, recognises their presence, then rises up to surmount and overcome them. Anything less than this will let you down.

4. Faith is not trying hard to believe

That is anxiety trying to look like faith. Harold Horton, in his book *The Gifts of the Spirit*, says of faith: "Faith is not grasping tight and clenching fists and furrowing brows and gritting teeth and shouting in a kind of hopeless hope, 'I *do* believe; I *will* believe.' Faith is absolute rest in God – absolutely knowing and absolutely trusting according to His gracious promises and commands."

There is a humorous touch to Paul's statement in Romans 16:12, which Moffatt translates in this way: "Salute Tryphaena and Tryphosa, who work hard in the Lord." I heard one preacher refer to them as "Brother Try" and "Sister Try" – sweating Christians who "work hard in the Lord". He went on to say that he would like to have changed their names to "Trustphaena and Trustphosa" who "accomplish much in the Lord"!

I meet many Christians who are almost on the point of exhaustion from struggling hard to believe. That is trying, not trusting. Faith is the easy, restful, fearless attitude of an infant reposing on its mother's breast – with no thought of fear, effort or uncertainty.

A young minister I know, whose ministry was failing because of trying too hard, was told by his church that they thought he should give up the ministry and return to secular employment. For three days he struggled over this, then God spoke to him and said, "Stop struggling – and let Me hold you." He did just that – he surrendered his ministry to God and, within weeks, became a new man with a new ministry. He passed from fighting to faith, from trying to trusting – and then "accomplished much in the Lord".

Problem of Positive Thinking

5. Faith is not positive thinking

It would be foolish to assert that positive thinking has no value, because there would be millions who could rise up and claim that its principles have helped them to build successful and productive lives.

The concept of positive thinking is based on the famous statement of Emerson: "A man *is* what he thinks about all the day long." When we think positively, we tend to act positively – a fact which can hardly be denied. Our thought processes are extremely powerful, and by determined and positive thinking we can lift ourselves out of poverty, overcome failure and conquer disabilities.

The difference between positive thinking and faith can be seen when we ask the question: Is our positive thinking in line with God's thinking? Our thoughts may be positive, but are they the thoughts on which God wants us to focus? It is perfectly possible to achieve great things through the power of positive thinking – make no mistake about that – but the tragedy is that we can think ourselves into situations where God may not wish us to go.

Many years ago, I talked to a millionaire in Georgia, USA, who told me that by the power of positive thinking, he had amassed a huge fortune. Then, with tears in his eyes, he said, "But I realise now that this was not the path that God wanted me to pursue." I am afraid that much of what passes as "faith" in Christian circles is nothing more than positive thinking – and positive thinking that is not in harmony with biblical thinking turns out to be nothing more than wishful thinking.

Presume nothing

We come now to what is perhaps the most important statement we have made so far:

6. Faith is not presumption

It is at this point that many come unstuck, for the line between presumption and faith is finely drawn and is often difficult to discern. Some of the greatest tragedies in the Church happen because people launch out on what they believe is faith, but which subsequent events show is nothing more than presumption. I have fallen down at this point many times in my life – and so, I imagine, have you.

A woman I knew, who was a diabetic, read these words in the

Scriptures one day: "I am the Lord, who heals you" (Exod. 15:26). She took this as a direct word from the Lord, and in "faith" gave up her insulin injections. Within three days she had died. Sadly, she acted in presumption and not in faith.

What then is presumption? Presumption is a subject that would take a whole book to exhaust, but basically it is a failure to differentiate between the general and the specific. The words, "I am the Lord, who heals you", is a general statement that shows God to be the healer of His people. How that statement is applied, however, must be approached with care. As a general principle, it is perfectly true that God delights to heal, but in some specific instances He may have good reasons for withholding healing.

Those who fasten on general principles, and fail to apply them prayerfully and carefully in specific situations, are in danger of acting, not in faith, but in presumption. And you do not need me to tell you that presumption has a great reputation for tragic endings.

Keep back thy servant also from presumptuous sins;
let them not have dominion over me! (Psa. 19:13, RSV)

Bible scholars point out that two different Greek words are used in the New Testament for "word". One is *logos*, which means "the word," and the other *rhema*, which means a *directed* word from God – a special word for a special situation. Faith comes as the result of a *rhema*, a specific word from the Lord, flowing into the *logos* – the general persuasion that "God has said". The *rhema* will not go beyond the *logos*, but it will stake its all on it.

For example, Naaman was the only person who was healed by dipping seven times in the Jordan, and only Peter walked on the Lake of Galilee. These miracles came as a result of God's direct word to specific individuals on specific occasions. The *rhema* of God became a faith-producing word. In Numbers 14:26–45 we see Israel moving presumptuously into battle against the Amalekites and the Canaanites. The result? A bitter defeat for the Israelites.

It's interesting that the word "presumed" used in Numbers 14 is precisely the same Hebrew word which Habakkuk uses to describe those who act in unbelief: *aphal* (Hab. 2:4). It means, as we saw, proud, puffed up, self-centred, conceited. The presumptuous person speaks whether God has spoken or not. He seeks to get God to do what he wants Him to do, irrespective of whether God wants to do it or not. Presumption is not faith: when presumption prevails, then death, not life, is the result.

Sadly and sometimes tragically, many things are confused with faith which are not the genuine article at all. Having examined what faith is not, we are ready now to look at what it is.

3

God's
perspective

"Now faith is being sure of what we hope for and certain of what we do not see." (Hebrews 11:1)

Over the years, I have come across many interesting and intriguing definitions of faith, but not one that matches the definition given in the opening verse of Hebrews 11. This, by the way, is the only definition of faith to be found in the Bible. There are, of course, many explanations and applications of faith in Scripture, but only one clear-cut definition. "Faith," says the writer to the Hebrews, "is being sure of what we *hope for* ..."

So then, faith begins with *hope*, which means, in this context, a *confident expectation*. Hope for what? Things not yet attained, things not yet in our possession. But what sort of things are we hoping for? Pause for a moment and ask yourself this pointed and personal question: What is the greatest longing of my life – my greatest hope?

Consider your answer carefully – for by it you will stand revealed. If you say that your greatest longing and hope is for a bigger house, a new car, a better job or greater financial security, then sadly, I have to tell you that you are a million miles off the mark. You are thinking on the level of mere dust, where, as a poet put it:

The earth of a dusty today,
Is the dust of an earthy tomorrow.

Faith begins, not with the hope of realising our self-centred interests, but with the highest interests of the universe, the realisation of Christian ideals, the compensation for the things which have to be endured and the ultimate victory of good over evil. And if you don't start there, you simply don't start!

Many Christians think that faith begins with the hope of a new house, greater financial security or perhaps a physical healing – but that is not so. It has something to do with those things, of course, but it doesn't begin there. Faith begins with the hope that there will come a time in human affairs when an even balance will be struck or, as a poet put it:

The far-off divine event
To which the whole creation moves.

In fact, the whole thrust of Hebrews ii is that when we live by faith, we have the solid hope that, though it may be through scourgings and mockings, perils and dangers, we shall arrive safe and secure in our Father's presence. What a hope!

Why is it necessary to focus on this ingredient of hope as being so vital to faith? Because it is only as we understand faith on its highest level that we can implement it on the lower levels. Faith has to be cultivated in the certain knowledge that God's long-range purpose is to right all wrongs and usher in His triumphant kingdom. The more that hope prevails in our hearts, the more certain will be our hope in God's ability to meet our personal and individual needs. If we are not assured of the highest, then how can we be assured of the lowest?

The long look

What was the single truth that nerved and nourished the heroes of faith listed in Hebrews 11? This: "These all died in faith, not having received what was promised, but having seen it and greeted it from afar ..." (v.13, RSV). "*Having seen it ... from afar*" – what an exciting phrase! They took the "long look" and saw that no matter what happened in the present, the future was fixed and certain.

Christians, above all others, ought to be people of the long view. Far too many of us, however, suffer from spiritual shortsightedness – we see no further than *today* – with its pressing personal needs and claims.

Can you see the point I am making? If we don't cultivate the "long look", and absorb the thrilling truth that God will one day bring all things to a good and glorious conclusion, then what basis of faith do we have for dealing with the day-to-day demands that press in upon us? We simply become the prisoners of today, rather than the pioneers of tomorrow.

When, however, we practise faith on the highest level, and are assured of the fact that we shall see the realisation of our ideals, the ultimate victory of good and compensation for every wrong, we have a focus for our faith that will equip us for handling anything that comes our way. When we continually practise the "long look", the things to hand will present little difficulty.

The sure and certain hope

Quietly the thought is shaping itself in our minds that if we are to have faith, then it must first be focused on the certain hope that, one day in the future, God is going to bring all things to a good and glorious conclusion. If we don't have this solid assurance in relation to the future, then we will never be able to practise the principles of faith in the here and now.

I have seen many Christians trip up at this point. They have little understanding or conviction about the certainty with which

God will wind up the affairs of His universe, and then wonder why they are unable to deal with the mountains of difficulties in their lives which, according to Jesus, their faith ought to be able to remove. If we can't trust God to work out His long-range purposes, how can we trust Him to work them out in the short term? It's all a matter of perspective.

I have mentioned before the story of the artist who said of his nature paintings: "I can get the picture right if I can get the sky right." Well, it's the same in this matter of faith – you have to get the sky right. Once you catch the sweep of God's mind and the glory of His eternal purposes, and become a part of them, then your faith finds a powerful focus. Your sky is right – and so the rest of the picture will be right.

Many Christians, however, get it the wrong way round. They start with the temporal and lose sight of the eternal. If we lose our perspective on eternity, we shall most certainly lose it in time – but when we are sure of heaven, we shall be sure of earth. It's as simple as that. Recognise this – once you have won the battle in the eternal realm, you will not lose it in the earthly realm.

Seeing the invisible

The second phrase in this definition from Hebrews 11:1 reads: "Faith is ... *the conviction of things not seen*" (RSV). It's easy to believe in things we can see, but not so easy to believe in the things we cannot see. Yet this is exactly where faith operates. We do not need faith to operate in the realm of things we can see; it is sight, not faith, that operates there. Doubtless we have all heard the phrase, "seeing is believing", but when we stop and examine it we find that, really, it is not true. Believing is being sure without seeing.

Faith operates in the realm of things the physical eye cannot see, and is able, as the writer to the Hebrews puts it, to "see the invisible". This is not a contradiction, but a paradox. A paradox is something that may *seem* contrary to reason, but is nevertheless true. The law of the road in Britain, for example, is a paradox. (For those readers not from Britain, I should explain that we drive on the left.) Did you ever learn this verse at school?

The law of the road is a paradox quite
And that you may tell by my song
If you go to the left, you are sure to go right
And if you go right, you go wrong!

The law of the road is a *perfect* paradox; apparently wrong, contrary to reason, but nevertheless true. So is faith a paradox. Faith sees the invisible, knows the unknowable, hears the inaudible, touches the intangible – fights in chains and rests in conflict. Not contradictory but paradoxical. And therefore true.

By faith a Christian "sees" the unseen. He is as conscious, if not more so, of the reality of the spiritual world around him as he is of the material objects which he handles day by day. The non-Christian puzzles over this and dismisses it as "crazy".

Speaking for myself, I am often more conscious of the spiritual world around me than I am of the word processor on which I am writing these lines. Faith has put me in touch with the ultimate reality – the kingdom of God. These realities, these unseen forces, which cannot be seen, measured, analysed or touched, are my life. To be without them now would not be life, but mere existence.

How aware are you of the reality of the "unseen"? Can you reach out by faith and become so conscious of the unseen spiritual world around you that all your fears are dispelled? If not, I pray that what happened to Elisha's servant (2 Kings 6:15–17) will happen to you today. The prophet prayed: "O Lord, open his eyes," and instantly the prayer was answered. How do we know? "Then the Lord opened the servant's eyes, and he looked and saw the hills full of horses and chariots of fire all round Elisha" (v.17).

If you knew – really knew – what spiritual forces are available to you through faith, you would never be afraid again. Do you remember how Charles Wesley put it?

Lo to faith's enlightened sight,
All the mountains flamed with light
Hell is nigh but God is nigher
Circling us with hosts of fire.

It is important to keep in mind that this definition of faith from Hebrews 11:1 is a *basic* one, and although we shall learn a lot more about faith as we go along, we shall never properly understand it unless we comprehend its intrinsic principles.

What, then, are the basic principles of faith? There are two – the first being *hope*. The word "hope" in Scripture, as we saw, is not something speculative, but something that is sure and certain. It is an unshakable confidence that the promises of God – "things hoped for" – whether they be for the distant future, or for the hours and days that lie immediately ahead, will be realised.

The second ingredient of faith is *awareness* – the sentient knowledge that within this physical universe there is something else present. And what is that "something else"? It is a spiritual world that is as real, if not more so, than the world which we relate to with our physical senses.

Faith always operates in the world of the unseen, for when we cease to believe in unseen things, hope dies. Putting these two basic ingredients together – and we must resist any temptation to go further than this at the moment – we come up with this as a working conclusion: Faith is an inner conviction that banks on the bona fide promises of God. It reaches out to the unseen, focuses upon it, grasps its reality and then acts upon it in the confidence that what God has said will inevitably come to pass.

Understanding **faith**

"By faith we understand that the universe was formed at God's command, so that what is seen was not made out of what was visible." (Hebrews 11:3)

The writer to the Hebrews, having given us a definition of faith, now proceeds to draw some interesting deductions from it – and it is these deductions which will now occupy our attention.

We begin right away with the first: "For by it [i.e. by *faith*] the elders obtained a good report" (Heb. 11:2, AV). The usual interpretation of this text is this: just as when we were at school and brought home a good report (hopefully) at the end of term, so did the spiritual leaders of the Old Testament era. Because they lived and acted by faith, they received the highest possible marks. Now I do not deny that this is a possible interpretation, but I do not believe it to be the correct one. The true interpretation of the text is best seen in the Amplified Bible, which reads thus: "For by faith ... the men of old had divine testimony borne to them and obtained a good report."

Notice these words carefully: "had divine testimony borne *to* them". Borne *to* them, not borne *about* them. The thought in the text is that these men were listening to a Voice that came to them with increasing power and conviction. This Voice, speaking with great authority, delineated, no doubt, the majestic truth that "the just shall live by faith".

Henry David Thoreau is famous for some words which, I think, help to illuminate the truth I am trying to bring out here. He said, "If a man is unable to keep step with his companions, perhaps it's because he hears the beat of a distant drummer." That is an exact description of faith: people walking through the world as though they are listening to another drum-beat. It was this that made the Old Testament saints so different from those around them. Does it make a difference to you?

Next we examine another deduction made by the writer to the Hebrews concerning faith: "By faith we understand that the universe was formed at God's command ..." (Heb. 11:3).

We focus first on the statement: "By faith we *understand*". What do we understand? The Amplified Version puts it thus: "By faith we understand that the worlds [during the successive ages] were framed (fashioned, put in order and equipped for their intended purpose) by the word of God ..." Notice carefully what this statement says. It does not say, "By faith we accept", or even "By faith we affirm", but "By faith we *understand* that the worlds were framed ... by the word of God". I wonder whether you recollect a line in one of Tennyson's poems which reads: "We have but faith; we cannot know."

I believe Tennyson to be entirely wrong in relation to this matter of faith. The truth is, when we have faith, *we can know*. The word "understand" simply means "an exercise of mind". Men who shut out God from their thinking, and then exercise their minds to try to discover the origin of the universe, almost reach mental exhaustion in their efforts to explain it.

I am not in any way decrying scientific study and research, but the man of faith does not depend upon scientific knowledge in order to understand the origin of the universe; he understands it by faith. We may not understand the scientific formulas that explain the structure of the universe, but we understand the simple but basic truth that it was all put together by our great and wonderful God.

Some scientists claim that the universe happened by chance. Quite frankly, even in my unconverted days I found that more difficult to believe and understand than the account given to us in Genesis. How could this universe come by chance into a cosmic orderliness that extends from a single atom to the farthest star, and controls everything in between? And how could this orderliness be maintained by chance throughout the long years of history? That would be an astounding materialistic miracle – universal chaos, by chance, giving birth to universal order! If anyone believes that, then he indeed believes in miracles – the very thing he condemns in the believer.

The genius of faith is that through it we can leap over the tortuous windings of reason, avoiding the need to grope by trial and error, and lay hold of the basic facts of the universe in a single moment. It pierces the illusions that tend to distract us, and brings us right to the point where we see things as they really are.

Science, that is science apart from God, cannot tell me how the universe began – or, for that matter, how it will end – but by faith I understand and know. Someday, perhaps after many painful decades, when man's reason has slowly and tortuously worked out some of the answers, mankind will find that faith could have brought them to the same place many years before. To trust God's Word may not be an easy path in this scientific age in which we live, but it is an absolutely sure one.

"Popping with excitement"

We have examined the first part of Hebrews 11:3: "By faith we understand that the universe was formed at God's command", and now we examine the final part: "so that what is seen was not made out of what is visible".

Can you see what it is saying? *We can never explain things which are seen until we come to understand the things that are unseen.* Perhaps you will be able to understand now why it is that so many scientists and philosophers struggle over the mysteries of the universe – they fail to recognise the existence of unseen things, and therefore they are unable *fully* to understand the meaning of the things that are visible. A scientist I once knew in Swansea, South Wales, who lectured at the university there, told me that prior to his conversion, he was greatly perplexed about the nature of creation. He said, "I felt as if I was looking at creation through a dark glass, and I tried as hard as I could to make the glass come clear, but it just wouldn't. Now, however, I can read creation like an open book. Almost every day a new secret unfolds itself. The universe is popping with excitement!"

Notice the contrast in his terms: before, "I was looking at creation through a dark glass"; now, "the universe is popping with excitement!" What made the difference? Conversion! When this scientist came by faith to the cross, he discovered something greater than creation – he discovered the Creator. And the more he understood God and fellowshipped with Him in the world of the unseen, the more clearly he came to understand the secrets of the material world around him.

"I knew ... all the time"

This brings me to a verse which strikes deeper than anything we have heard so far. It is this: " ... anyone who comes to him must believe that he exists and that he rewards those who earnestly seek him" (Heb. 11:6).

Have you noticed how the Bible never argues for the existence of God? It assumes it. Even our Lord Himself never argued for the existence of His heavenly Father – He merely proceeded in all His teachings and His mighty miracles to act on this assumption. If we come to God we must believe that He is – that He exists.

Ah, says someone, but that is the hardest and most difficult thing to do – *to believe that God exists*. How often that is affirmed. I disagree – in fact I would go further and say that to believe in God is the easiest thing in the world. It requires effort to *disbelieve*, but it requires little effort to believe. Everyone born into this world starts out by believing God exists. It is only when they are trained not to believe, that they come to the place of declaring God does not exist.

That is why children have very little difficulty with the concept of God. You would think, bearing in mind that God is unseen, that children would stumble over this – but they don't. I am thinking as I write of Miss Sullivan, the woman who cared for Helen Keller – a child who was deaf, dumb and blind. She approached Bishop Phillip Brooks to help her spell out to Helen the concept and nature of God. As he did so – in sign language – Helen Keller's face became radiant. She replied, "I see what you mean, *but I have known that all the time."*

Perhaps my statement that it takes effort to disbelieve in God was quite a revelation to you – but believe me, it is true. Tertullian, one of the Church Fathers, said on one occasion, "The soul is naturally Christian." What did he mean? Did he mean that conversion and regeneration are unnecessary? No, he meant that the soul is created in such a way that, left to itself and without the influences of secularism and atheism, it will come to the conclusion that the words "created by him and for him" (see Col. 1:16) are imprinted on it.

For many years now, HMV, the music company, have used as a trademark a picture of a dog listening to "his master's voice" in the horn of an old-fashioned phonograph.

Is not this a parable of humanity listening to its *Master's voice* which is inherent in the nature of things? If we would listen we would hear His voice everywhere – particularly in our inner being, for we were made by Him, designed by Him and will never be at peace until we are indwelt by Him.

Some time ago someone sent me a book written by an atheist

and entitled *Seven Reasons Why I Disbelieve in the Existence of God*. As I browsed through it, I was staggered at the effort the writer made to explain God away. It is only in the minds of those who have been trained and brainwashed by a secular society that the existence of God is doubted or denied. Even then, they have to be careful or they are apt to make a slip, as Khrushchev did, when he once said: "Thank God I'm an atheist"!

The great Rewarder

We are seeing that faith begins when we believe in the existence of God, for "anyone who comes to him must believe that he exists". If we want to approach Him, then we must begin at this point. But it is possible to believe that He exists and still not make contact with Him. That is why this second statement is so vitally important: "anyone who comes to him *must believe ... that he rewards those who earnestly seek him*" (Heb. 11:6).

Once we believe that God exists, and that He rewards those who come to Him by revealing Himself to them, then our feet stand firmly on the bedrock of faith. Here, by the way, is the answer to the question I am often asked: What about the heathen who have never heard the gospel? Well, even they have the opportunity to exercise faith, for faith, at its simplest level, is *believing that God exists and that He rewards those who seek Him.*

Anyone who believes this, and obeys that revelation, despite all difficulties and obstacles, will be brought to a knowledge of the truth of Jesus Christ. An African Christian tells how, one night, he looked up at the stars and said, "God, I know You exist, that is all – please help me to get to know You better." The Holy Spirit guided him through the jungle for a period of six weeks until at last he came to a village where he heard a missionary tell the story of the cross. He responded to the invitation that was given, and accepted Christ as his Lord and Saviour. As Dr Sam Shoemaker, the outstanding American Episcopalian preacher, used to say, "When coming to God, use the little faith you have and God will give you more." I know that is true. It has worked for me and I know it will work for you.

5

Examples
of **faith**

"By faith Abel offered God a better sacrifice than Cain ..."
(Hebrews 11:4)

The writer to the Hebrews, having given us a definition of faith
and his inspired deductions concerning it, goes on in chapter
11 to show us how faith works. He is well aware that it is a lot
easier to get hold of abstract truth when it is "fleshed out" in a
person's life so, turning to the stream of history, he selects a few
living illustrations.

The list of names which he records – beginning with Abel and
ending with Jesus – has been called by someone "The
Westminster Abbey of the Bible", because so many heroes of faith
are enshrined here.

The question arises: Did the writer to the Hebrews pull these
names out of the air at random, or was there some special and
significant reason underlying his choice? He selects them, so I
believe, under the inspiration and guidance of the Holy Spirit,
because *each one illustrates a particular aspect and characteristic of
faith.* Our task, as we look at each of these characters in turn, is to

test ourselves to see how many of their distinguishing marks of faith are present in our own lives.

Worshipping, walking and living by faith

The first name we encounter is that of Abel. Why Abel? Because it is in him that the primary note of faith is struck, namely that *in coming to God, we must be prepared to lay aside independent judgment and take God's way in all things.* Cain believed that "one way is as good as another", and brought fruit and vegetables as his offering. As a result, Cain was rejected. Abel believed God, and brought the offering he knew God wanted – *a blood* sacrifice. Faith recognises that the only way into God's presence is by way of an atoning sacrifice. Because Abel was the first man to learn that truth, he is still speaking to us – and we still need to listen.

Enoch is the second name on this inspired list of the heroes of faith (Heb. 11:5). He is one of the only two men in the Old Testament who went to heaven without dying – the other being Elijah (2 Kings 2:11). Enoch walked so closely with God that he found a fellowship which death could not interrupt.

As one little girl put it: "One day Enoch walked so far with God that God said, 'Look, Enoch, it's too far for you to go back now: come on home with Me.' So he walked on home with God." Enoch has become forever a picture of what death is to the Christian – not a termination, but a transition. Faith fears nothing – least of all death.

Next on the list is Noah (Heb. 11:7). He was, without doubt, one of the greatest men in the Old Testament. Noah believed that God was in charge of history and was prepared to bank everything on that belief. When God told him that He was about to judge the world by a flood, Noah believed Him and set about informing the people of his day about the imminent danger. The response he got was one of ridicule and scorn: "Fancy building a boat hundreds of miles from the nearest ocean," they would have said. By faith, however, Noah continued his preaching for 120 years. He did the thing for which he saw no earthly reason – just because God had commanded it – thus giving God a vantage point for a strategic movement in history. Faith acts on what God says, even though circumstances seem to say that it is all futile. Noah was led on by faith to become an *heir of righteousness*. This is precisely what God is calling you and me to do – to witness by faith when everything seems contradictory, and to carry on the great march of righteousness towards its consummation.

Abraham – the friend of God

Of the greatness of Abraham there can be no question. He is held in high esteem, not only by Christianity but also by two other world religions – Judaism and Islam. In this classic chapter on faith, the writer has more to say about Abraham than about anyone else, implying that the patriarch stands head and shoulders above all the rest in this brief but illustrious list (Heb. 11:8).

Three great movements of faith are referred to in his story. 1. Abraham obeying God's call (Gen. 12:1–9); 2. Abraham sojourning in the land of promise (Gen. 13:14–18); and 3. Abraham offering up his son Isaac (Gen. 22:1–18). Someone has summed up his life in this way: faith *obeying*, faith *onlooking* and faith *offering*. Each movement of faith is significant, but the overall message that comes through Abraham's life is that of unswerving obedience: he obeyed "even though he did not know where he was going".

Here is a man who set out on a journey with an unknown destination – simply because God asked him to. He gave up the security of a house, settled for a lifetime in a tent and undertook a march without a map. What incredible obedience! No wonder he has been called "the father of the faithful". Abraham may not have known where he was going, but he knew with Whom he was going. And – as I am sure you know – what a difference that makes!

By faith – anticipate

Isaac, Jacob and Joseph are linked together in the list of heroes of faith (Heb. 11:20–22). There is a special reason why the writer to the Hebrews links these three names together, and when we understand that, we shall see more clearly the particular aspect of faith which he is seeking to illustrate.

It is intriguing that, in each case, the illustrations of faith given are drawn from the latter part of the patriarchs' lives. The writer makes no reference to the earlier part of their lives, but states that in their closing days these three great men demonstrated their faith in a remarkable way. Isaac and Jacob, who knew that God intended to build nations from their descendants, prayed in anticipation of what God had promised, and blessed their children on that basis. Joseph also, when he was dying, saw hundreds of years ahead to the coming exodus from Egypt, and he made arrangements by *faith* for his bones to be buried in the promised land. Thus he symbolised his conviction that God was going to do exactly as He had said – and, in the course of time, that was the way it happened. The children of Israel took Joseph's bones with them, and after forty years in the wilderness finally buried them in Canaan. That was most certainly the longest funeral procession in history!

The characteristic of faith illustrated by these three great patriarchs is that faith *anticipates*. It moves towards a clearly expected event in the future. As Kierkegaard said, "Life can be understood backwards, but it can only be lived forwards." Faith not only believes what God has promised, but looks with delight and anticipation for that which is to come.

We come next to two *unnamed* heroes of faith – the parents of Moses.

By faith Moses' parents hid him ... By faith he left Egypt ...
(Heb. 11:23,27)

We know, of course, from Exodus 6:20, that their names were Amram and Jochebed. When we read the Exodus story, the impression we get is that of loving parents acting out of concern for their baby, but here the writer says there was another ingredient present in their action – *faith*.

When Amram and Jochebed made that ark out of bulrushes, placed their precious baby in it and cast it upon the waters, it was a great and venturesome faith in the presence of apparently the most hopeless circumstances. They believed that the Almighty would somehow overrule the king's decision, and they ventured their all on that conviction. Thus they illustrated another characteristic of faith – faith *ventures*.

Next the writer focuses on Moses himself. Most Christians are familiar with the wonderful story of this great man's life – a life which spanned a period of 120 years. The significant characteristic of faith which Moses illustrates is undoubtedly this – faith *evaluates*.

In Moses we see the mental process which faith follows. First – "he refused" – to be known as the son of Pharaoh's daughter. But on what basis did he refuse? By "choosing". How did he come to choose? By considering, or "accounting". See the mental process here. The word "accounting" means balancing things in order to come to a decision, putting this by the side of that, and weighing the evidence on both sides. He weighed the wealth of Egypt and the prestige of royalty against the possibility of being an instrument in the hands of the Living God, and by faith "he regarded disgrace for the sake of Christ as of greater value than the treasures of Egypt" (v.26).

Rahab and the Israelites

We come now to the last few references to faith which we find listed in Hebrews 11, the first of which concerns the nation of Israel. Two incidents are selected – first, the crossing of the Red Sea (Heb. 11:29) and second, the conquering of Jericho (Heb. 11:31).

Despite all the failures of Israel, these two occasions show them demonstrating a faith that produced an amazing deliverance.

That's another thing faith does – it pays no attention to impossibilities and believes in miracles. As one hymn writer has put it:

Faith, mighty faith, the promise sees
And looks to God alone
Laughs at impossibilities and cries,
"It shall be done."

Next, and in startling contrast to all the other names on this list, comes that of Rahab. Why, we ask ourselves, should a pagan prostitute be placed alongside such heroes of faith as Abel, Enoch, Noah, Abraham and the others? The answer, of course, is because she demonstrated great faith. Rahab had obviously heard much about the approaching army of Israel (Josh. 2:10) – how God had opened up the Red Sea for them, their conquest of the Amorites and so on – and, as a result of all this, a great conviction possessed her soul.

Here it is in her own words: "For we have heard how the Lord dried up the water of the Red Sea before you ... for the Lord your God is he who is God in heaven above and on earth beneath" (Josh. 2:10–11, RSV). As a result of this conviction, she forsook her pagan religion, risked her life on behalf of the spies and put her faith firmly in God. Faith risks everything once it is sure of God.

The faith of others

We come now to the close of this great chapter on faith, and the writer finishes with a burst of exploits and deeds that is vibrant with power, poignant in its account of sufferings and challenging in its revelation of triumph. The temptation he faces is to take each name and deal with them one by one but, as he explains, "time would fail me to tell" (v.32, RSV). He wants us to know that although he is running out of time, he is not running out of names, nor has he come even near to exhausting his theme.

One word seems to stand out in this impressive passage and is, I believe, worthy of special mention: it is the word "others". Who are these "others"? Obviously the multitudes of people who, down the ages, have lived their lives by the principle of faith. And that, if you are truly one of Christ's disciples, includes you.

Someone has called this chapter the "unfinished chapter of the Bible". It is easy to see why. God is still calling men and women to live by faith, and the list will go on being added to until the last moment of recorded time. What is more, if we venture our all on the Living God, we too shall someday have our names added to this illustrious list of heroes and be counted among those who received "a good report".

The final sentences of this passage are designed to bring us face to face with the least spectacular, but the most important aspect of faith, namely that faith *perseveres*. "These all died in faith, not having received what was promised" (Heb. 11:13, RSV). They were looking for more than their own personal satisfaction – they were waiting to see God's purposes being fulfilled on earth. And though that may not be the most spectacular exercise of faith, it is by far the most important.

6

Focusing your **gaze**

"Therefore, since we are surrounded by such a great cloud of witnesses ... let us run with perseverance ... Let us fix our eyes on Jesus, the author and perfecter of our faith." (Hebrews 12:1–2)

Having spent some time meditating on Hebrews 11, we move on now to focus on the opening verses of Hebrews 12. In a sense we are obliged to do this, for without an understanding of Hebrews 12, the great argument of the previous chapter is somewhat lost.

We begin by asking ourselves: Who are the "cloud of witnesses" to whom the writer refers here? Some think they consist of those who have died and have gone to heaven, and who are now leaning over the battlements of heaven watching to see how we are doing. But the text is quite clear – it refers not to watching, but to witnessing. The thought in the writer's mind is that the examples of faith he has given us in Hebrews 11 are saying something important to us – they are testifying to us, they are witnessing to us about the force and potency of faith.

In the light of this, he bids us to "throw off everything that hinders" ("every weight", RSV). What are these "weights"? Well, clearly the things that hinder us from running freely. Shall I name some? No, for what might be a weight or hindrance to me might not be to you. But perhaps, despite what I have just said, I will name just one – the weight of trying to find out what other people's weights are!

He encourages us also to get rid of "sin which so easily entangles". What is that? It can be expressed in one word – *unbelief*. If you have ever read through the book of Hebrews, you will find that this word, in one form or another, is mentioned time and again. It is the sin of failing to take God's Word seriously. Unbelief kept a whole nation out of the promised land for forty years. Don't, I beg you, let it keep you from knowing and experiencing mighty and unlimited power!

After we have learnt to take God's Word seriously – what then? This: "Let us run with patient endurance and steady and active persistence ... the race that is set before us" (Amplified). Notice yet again the writer to the Hebrews underlines the most significant characteristic of faith – *perseverance* – which means "keeping on no matter what happens". But how? By looking to Jesus, the Author and Finisher of our faith. The phrase "fix our eyes on Jesus" used here needs some amendment, because the phrase, by itself, does not contain the real meaning of the writer's words. Listen to how the Amplified renders it. "Looking away from all that will distract ... to Jesus."

The point the writer is making here is this – although the illustrations of faith which he has used in Hebrews 11 are potent and powerful, they must be seen as illustrations, and *not* as examples. We are not to fix our eyes upon the saints of the past, in the Old Testament or in the New, but we are to look away from them and focus our gaze upon Jesus. There is not one out of all those named in Hebrews 11 who could be described as a perfect example of faith. Abel needed an atoning sacrifice in order to come into God's presence. Enoch walked with the Lord, but for the first

65 years of his life he lived on the mediocre spiritual level of his times. Abraham more than once turned aside from the simple pathway of faith. But with Jesus it was different. He is the perfect example; our example *par excellence*. Dr Campbell Morgan used to say that there were times when he wished that the lives of the saints had never been written. He claimed that the temptation we face when reading about them is to gaze at them, rather than glance at them. Warming to this theme one night in his pulpit at Westminster Chapel, he shouted, "Quit looking at the saints of the Christian era. Look off; there is just one point where your vision may be fully satisfied – 'looking off unto Jesus'."

When the saints of the past are examined under the microscope, they are shown to be shot through with failure and imperfection. When Jesus is put under the microscope, however, there is but one verdict: He is vindicated by *all* that He does. In America many years ago, a note was struck over the radio each day from Washington by which the nation could tune its instruments. It was known as a 440 – the standard note. Everything that was not tuned to it was discordant. In Jesus, the standard note for faith – and, for that matter, everything else – has been struck. Everything that is tuned to Him is in harmony, and everything that is not is discordant.

The Head of the procession

In the phrase, "Jesus the author and perfecter [finisher, AV] of our faith", it is significant that the word "our" is not present in the Greek, and therefore the text should read thus: "Jesus the author and perfecter of faith". The writer is talking here about the principle of faith, and he declares that the principle is only fully seen and fully demonstrated in Jesus. Can you see the difference this makes to the text? Take the word "author" also. A better translation of the original Greek word used here is "file-leader". It does not mean, as some translations put it, "originator" or "beginner". It means the one who takes precedence, the head of the procession, leading it in revelation. What the writer to the Hebrews is attempting to bring out in this word is the picture of Jesus leading the great procession of those who witness to the power of faith. As we have worked our way through these wonderful chapters of Hebrews, we have seen some marvellous and moving illustrations of faith. It is indeed a wonderful procession that spans the ages from Abel to Jesus: but look, hold your breath, for One races past them all and makes His way right to the front of the procession. And who is He? It is Jesus, the File-leader, the One who has total pre-eminence. We have seen some pretty impressive illustrations of faith in Hebrews 11, but not one who can come up to Jesus. Alongside Him, the great heroes of faith, such as Enoch, Noah and Abraham, pale into insignificance. Jesus is not just another great hero of faith. He is the *greatest*!

When we glanced at the great heroes of faith in Hebrews 11, we saw many fine illustrations of faith. We saw Abel worshipping by faith, Enoch walking by faith and Noah working by faith. Now turn your gaze from them and look at Jesus. What do you see? No one worshipped God, walked or worked for God as did Jesus. In these three capacities alone, see how He moves to the head of the procession.

Then we looked at Abraham and saw his faith at work as he "obeyed and went, even though he did not know where he was going" (Heb. 11:8). Again, turn your eyes away and look to Jesus – and what do you find? Never was there such an obedience as His. It brought Him, not into an unknown country, but face to face with a grisly cross.

We looked at Joseph who, after his death, was embalmed and laid to rest. So was Jesus – but because of who He was and what He had wrought through His life, the grave could not hold Him. He arose! We also looked at Moses who, because of his sin, was forbidden to enter the promised land. Jesus, however, not only accomplished an exodus far greater than anything Moses ever dreamed of, but actually brought Moses to:

Stand with glory wrapt around
On the hills he never trod
And speak of the strife that won our life
With the incarnate Son of God.

The Vindicator of faith

Having seen what the writer to the Hebrews had in mind when he spoke of Jesus as the File-leader of faith, we turn now to consider what lies behind the meaning of the word "finisher" or "perfecter". The real meaning of this word in the original Greek is "vindicator". Jesus is not only pre-eminent as the File-leader of faith – the One who leads the procession – but He is pre-eminent also as the Vindicator of faith – the One who establishes it as an abiding and eternal principle.

Comb the record of Jesus' days on earth, and not once do you ever find His faith wavering. He demonstrated an unshakable confidence in God His Father: "Whatever the Father does the Son also does" (John 5:19).

Faith in God leads inevitably to faith in man. Faith in man? Perhaps you find that difficult to accept. I do not know what you think of man, but I know what Jesus thought of him. He thought he was worth dying for. "The Cross for evermore," said one great theologian, "indicates the value that Jesus put upon man." What does God see in you and me? I do not rightly know. Perhaps it is His image in us, the hallmark of the divine, which, though blurred and damaged, is yet worthy of redemption.

Whatever it was, we know this – Jesus believed in man. His faith, however, was not only in God and man, but also faith in the future. He looked forward with confidence to the day when all the nations would be gathered before Him, and He would judge the world. Cast your mind back now to the text with which we began this book: "The just shall live by his faith" (Hab. 2:4, AV). Now ask yourself: Has Jesus vindicated that principle? Has He illustrated and exemplified it in a way that puts it beyond all possibility of misunderstanding? My heart says "Yes". How about yours?

"Who for the joy set before him"

We have now to consider this powerful passage from Hebrews 12: "Who for the joy set before him endured the cross, scorning its shame, and sat down at the right hand of the throne of God" (Heb. 12:2).

First we consider the phrase, "who for the joy set before him". What was this "joy" of which the writer speaks here? Was it His return to heaven? I think not. Faith, as we saw earlier, is confidence in "things hoped for, the evidence of things not seen" (AV). The vision that sustained our Lord was not merely that of getting back to His Father's throne, but of re-establishing in the universe the rule and reign of God.

In order to achieve that, however, a pathway had to be trodden: "Jesus ... endured the cross, scorning its shame" (v.2). Do you know of any phrase more full of infinite majesty and beauty than that? Nothing was more shameful than dying upon a cross, yet Jesus willingly gave Himself to it in order that you and I might be redeemed. I don't know about you, but a God like this can have my heart for ever!

Now we reach the culminating phrase: He "sat down at the right hand of the throne of God". Try and write that sentence against any of the names in the list of heroes of faith in Hebrews 11 – and what happens? It just doesn't fit! This statement can only be applied to Jesus. As we see Him seated there on His Father's throne, we cannot help but realise that, in words like this, faith has its last and unanswerable argument.

So let us focus our gaze on *Him* – and on no one else. We can glance at others, but we must concentrate on Him. Let this word sink deep into your heart: "Looking away from all that will distract to Jesus."

7

Questions
of **faith**

"For it is by grace you have been saved, through faith – and this not from yourselves, it is the gift of God." (Ephesians 2:8)

Having examined the importance and the nature of faith, we turn to consider some of the questions which arise whenever the subject of faith is discussed. It is impossible to deal with every question in one section, but we will look at the ones which are most often asked.

The first is this: Is there any difference between the faith we use in our natural lives and the faith we use in believing God? Our key verse from Ephesians 2 tells us that faith is one of God's gifts to us. When He created us, He built into our personalities the ability and capacity to believe. Belief is a habit of life: we have to believe to live.

In a sense, we can't go through a single day without faith. When we board a bus we have faith – faith that the driver will take us safely where we want to go. When we go to a restaurant we have faith – faith that the food is wholesome and properly prepared. When we send our children to school, we have faith – faith that the teachers will not poison their minds.

The reason why people do not use this God-given ability to believe in Christ is because, as the scripture says, Satan has "blinded the minds of the unbelieving" (2 Cor. 4:4, NASB). If I understand conversion correctly, what happens is this – through anointed preaching or witnessing, the Holy Spirit unfolds to the mind the reality of the gospel. Once this is understood, the individual then reaches out by faith to take hold of Christ – and is saved. Conversion is a combination of the human and the divine. It is both receptivity and activity. You do it – and He does it. Your personality is not stifled – because *you* believe – but *He* is still the One who saves.

Another question which is often asked is this: If every man has been given a measure of faith, why do we need an additional gift of faith as described in 1 Corinthians 12:9?

The faith spoken of in this chapter is a special kind of faith which is to be used for supernatural purposes. The list which Paul gives us here consists of nine "special abilities", as the Living Bible puts it in verse 4, which can be divided into three groups, with three gifts in each.

The first group of three enables a person supernaturally to *know* – the word of wisdom, word of knowledge and discerning of spirits. The second group enables a person supernaturally to *do* – faith, working of miracles and gifts of healing. The third group enables a person supernaturally to *speak* – tongues, interpretation and prophecy.

What, then, is the "special ability" called "faith" and how does it work? It is a divine gift, given only to certain people or on certain occasions, in order to accomplish supernatural exploits. Paul, I believe, demonstrated this gift in Acts 27:22 when he decreed, by faith, that there would be "no loss of life among you, but only of the ship" (RSV).

Although every Christian has faith – that is, *individual* faith – God has made it possible for us to have access to a supernatural realm that is beyond our ability to conceive. This kind of faith, when it operates through certain members of the Body of Christ, issues forth in mighty signs, wonders and miracles. How sad that, with such a need for God's power to be seen at work today, this gift is not more in evidence.

Faith versus *the* faith

Another question that is often asked when the subject of faith comes up is this: how does one understand the difference in Scripture between the phrases "faith" and "*the* faith"? Faith has to do with believing: *the* faith has to do with beliefs.

Acts chapter 6 verse 7 shows that, following the descent of the Holy Spirit at Pentecost, the Church began to emphasise certain beliefs which came to be recognised as the basis of the Christian faith. So clear was their emphasis on such things as the birth, life, death, resurrection and ascension of our Lord that these doctrines, as well as others, became the foundation of the faith.

When Paul returned to Lystra, Iconium and Antioch in order to encourage the converts, we are told that he exhorted them to "continue in the faith, and that we must through much tribulation enter into the kingdom of God" (Acts 14:22, AV). Again Jude, in the third verse of his short epistle, says, "I felt I had to write and urge you to contend for the faith".

The phrase "*the* faith", when used in the New Testament, has reference to the systematic declaration of certain biblical truths which form the corporate basis of our beliefs as Christians. The tragedy, of course, is that with some, the doctrines become the basis for their individual faith, rather than a personal commitment and trust in Christ. If we mistake *the* faith for individual faith, we are in deep trouble. When I ask myself why it is that, at this time in our history, so many of our theologians are attempting to tamper with the faith, the conclusion I come to is that perhaps it is because they are not sure of the basis of their own personal faith.

Faith and faithfulness

Another question that is asked concerning faith is this: Is there any difference between ordinary faith and the faith which is listed as one of the fruit of the Spirit in Galatians 5? Although the word used here is the same Greek word which almost everywhere else is translated "faith" (Greek: *pistis*), most translators claim that the best translation of the word is not "faith" but "faithfulness".

In fact, most translations use the word "faithfulness" in preference to "faith", although some prefer the word "fidelity". The thought that flows through this word is not so much of a person being strong in his ability to believe, but one who is trustworthy, reliable and dependable.

Faith – that is, individual faith – is the venturing of the whole personality in trusting one who is worthy. Faith – the gift – is the supernatural ability to believe for a miraculous manifestation of God's power. Faithfulness, or fidelity, is one of the nine characteristics which grow in the life of a believer as the natural outflow of the Spirit who abides within. The first two of these characteristics have a miracle quality and not a moral one – the third has a moral quality and not a miracle one.

It is interesting to note that when Paul speaks of "the works of the flesh" in verses 19–21 of Galations 5 (AV), he calls them "works", but when he speaks of the moral qualities in the life of the believer, he refers to them as "fruit". What is the difference? "Works" points to something manufactured, not natural; "fruit" points to something that grows as a natural outcome. Every Christian has faith, but not all Christians have faithfulness. Faith needs work if it is to grow; faithfulness does not need work, but is the natural outcome of abiding in the Vine.

Faith versus works

This leads us to what many have seen as a contradiction in Scripture: If faith is of such prime importance, why is it that James lays such an emphasis on works?

When the apostle James wrote these words, " ... so faith without works is dead also" (James 2:26, NKJ) he began a controversy among Christians which has gone on for centuries. Personally I regard it as no more than a storm in a teacup. The problem is caused when his words are compared with those of the apostle Paul in Galatians 2:16: "A man is not justified by works of the law but through faith in Jesus Christ ... because by works of the law shall no one be justified" (RSV). Putting James in opposition to Paul is a popular pastime with some Christians, and on one occasion even the great Martin Luther fell into this trap. On one occasion he referred to the epistle of James as "the epistle of straw".

James and Paul, both writing under the inspiration of the Holy Spirit, do not contradict each other – they complement each other. Paul points out that works cannot result in faith, while James points out that faith must inevitably result in works.

James does not deprecate faith, for, as he says, "Abraham believed God, and it was credited to him as righteousness" – but he goes on to make the point that "a person is justified by what he does and not by faith alone" (v.24). Contradictory? It may appear to be so, but actually it is not.

James' point is that the only faith which can be accounted as righteous is the faith that comes to fruition in works. If works are the basis of our faith, then it is competitive, but if works flow out of faith, it is complementary. Works can never produce faith, but faith inevitably produces works.

Positive confession

My correspondence shows there is one question which is often asked concerning faith. It goes like this: In order to have faith, must we not do more than believe? Should we not also speak out words of positive confession?

The thinking behind this question is related to a form of

Christian teaching known as "Positive Confession": that we shall have whatever our mouth speaks out, so when we refuse to accept a negative situation and declare it to be a positive one, this will generate sufficient faith to bring about a dramatic change in our circumstances.

Another teaching, closely related to this, states that one should testify to one's healing whether the facts support it or not, since testifying "before the fact" generates the faith to produce the fact. Some who take this to extremes claim that the abandoning of all medical assistance is an act that also generates faith.

There can be little doubt that faith and confession are linked together in Scripture. We see it when Jesus is giving the disciples a lesson in faith-filled praying (Mark 11:12–14, 20–25): "... whoever says to this mountain, 'Be removed ...' ... he will have whatever he says" (Mark 11:23 NKJ).

Jesus often spoke out in faith to situations. He spoke to a tree and it withered; He spoke to a storm and it ceased; He spoke to a corpse and it came to life.

The important thing to remember, however, is this: *confession does not create faith, but only releases it.* The words "he will have whatever he says" are dependent, not merely on what we say, but on the principle "Have faith in God". It is only after faith is present that it can be confessed. Positive confession is fine as long as it is used to release faith, and not create it.

Faith and prosperity

We look at one more question which is also extremely popular. It is this: If every believer used his faith to become prosperous, would not this convince unbelievers of the truth of the gospel?

This question arises out of another over-emphasis in today's Church – the issue of "prosperity". This teaching states that "when we are rightly related to God's principles and know how to exercise our faith, then we can have everything we want – in abundance". The philosophy underlying this teaching has been expressed by its exponents in phrases such as, "You possess what you confess", or "Name it and claim it".

Has God given us the ability to believe simply in order to get everything we want? I doubt it. God has clearly promised to supply all our needs (Phil. 4:19), but it is our *needs* that are guaranteed, not our wants. Those who use Philippians 4:19 to advocate "prosperity" should read the context: "I know what it is to be in need, and I know what it is to have plenty" (Phil. 4:12).

Paul willingly accepted all levels of God's provision for his life, fully realising that God would give him what was best for him at the time. I do not believe in the "poverty syndrome" advocated by many Christians – that the more we skimp on things the more spiritual we are – but neither do I believe in the possession of things for their own sake. It needs a special kind of person to handle prosperity. Those who push God hard to let them become prosperous may find that He lets them have their way, finishing up like Israel in the wilderness: "And he gave them their request; but sent leanness into their soul" (Psa. 106:15, AV).

Steps into **faith**

"We ought always to thank God for you ... because your faith is growing more and more ..." (2 Thessalonians 1:3)

Having seen something of the importance and nature of faith, we come now to the most important section of our meditations in which we look at some of the steps we must take if our faith is to expand and develop.

1. See that faith is not something that is fixed, but something that can develop and grow

Many Christians never get far in the development of their faith because they see it as something fixed and final and thus they have no expectation of growth. They point to the text: "God has dealt to each one a *measure* of faith" (Rom. 12:3, NKJ), and infer from this that our calling is to go through life functioning within our appointed and preordained circle.

But take another look at the text which is at the top of this page – this time in a different translation: "My brothers ... I always thank God for you ... *Your faith has made such strides*" (Phillips).

The Greek word used here is *huperauxano*, which means "to increase above the ordinary degree". I consider the belief that "we are given a fixed measure of faith and cannot expect it to increase" to be one of the most injurious of all the errors in the Christian Church today.

A missionary who found it difficult to grow trees in his garden was told by an expert, "Dig a very deep pit, put in a layer of fertilizer, then one of ordinary earth, then another layer of fertilizer, followed again by a layer of earth – and so on to the top." This, he said, gives the growing tree something to reach after. Its roots get to one level, and feel the call of the deeper richness. In the same way, your faith must be rooted in the truth that you are designed to be a growing person, or else it will remain dwarfed and immature.

Now that we have established the fact that faith can be developed, we are ready for the next step:

2. Make a conscious decision to give yourself to the task of cultivating your faith – and do it today

Someone has defined prayer as "constantly bringing the whole of life into the light of God's presence for cleansing and decision". Note the word "constantly", for that is the secret. You prayed at the opening of this book: "Lord, increase my faith." Now, in the light of what you have seen in Scripture and the challenges you have faced, it is time to firm up that prayer in an act of positive decision. "Character *is* decision," said a famous philosopher. So decide now to give yourself fully to this task.

Cultivation of faith does not mean trying in your natural strength. The essence of cultivation is relaxation. You will never be a good musician if you try too hard – you must let go and let the music get into your fingertips, so that you do not play the music, but the music plays through you. It is the same with God. Don't use Him – let Him use you. Then you will be able to say with Walter Rauschenbusch, "My faith grows in the great quiet of God".

I like the way Moffatt translates 2 Peter 1:5: " ... furnish your faith with resolution." Note that faith is first, and resolution second. Christianity is not primarily resolution, a whipping up of the will. It is primarily faith – a surrender of the will. Faith is not struggling and striving: it is letting go and trusting. Once you fasten on God and you are linked to His endless power, then you can add resolution, for resolution is not anxious fretting, but a restful, confident reposing on God's infinite resources.

Keeping the right balance

A further step we must take in order to develop and cultivate our faith is this:

3. Get a proper perspective on the issue of how much God wants to do in your life, and how much He wants you to do

I am afraid that here, once again, we must face that thorny question of the sovereignty of God and the freedom of man. It is, however, an unavoidable issue, and one that relates directly to our ideas about faith. Many Christians, I find, have unbalanced views about these two concepts and get bogged down in their attempts to live a vibrant and effective life of faith.

If you are overbalanced on the issue of God's sovereignty then you will tend to sit back and let God do it all. If you are overbalanced on the issue of the freedom of the human will, then you will try to do it all yourself – and get nowhere. Error, more often than not, is truth out of balance.

God built an amazing faculty into us when He designed us with the ability to believe and trust, for faith is trust in another and yet it is an attitude of our own. It therefore develops self-reliance and other-reliance at one and the same time. If it were mere passivity, as some believe, it would not develop self-reliance. If it were mere activity, as others believe, it would not develop other-reliance.

This truth, I believe, is written into such statements as "According to your faith will it be done to you" and "Your faith has healed you". God retains His place as Creator, but invites us to create with Him and become, in a sense, mini-creators. God *develops* us as He gives to us.

Another step we must take if we are to grow and develop in faith is this:

4. Think long and often about the evidences of God's goodness and care

Have you ever noticed how, in the Scriptures, faith and thinking are linked together? We see it, for example, in Matthew 6:25–34. Dr Martyn Lloyd-Jones claims that faith is primarily ... *thinking*. Does that surprise you? Well, listen to what he says about this passage:

That is what Jesus is attempting to show here: that faith requires thought. "Look at the birds," says Jesus ... "*think* about them ... draw your deductions. Look at the flowers ... *think* about them ... draw your deductions. Look at the grass in the fields ... *think* about it ... draw your deductions." The whole trouble with a person of little faith is that he doesn't *think*. He allows circumstances to bludgeon him, and fails to consider the evidences of God's goodness and care. (*Studies in the Sermon on the Mount*, IVP)

This principle can be applied, not only in considering the way God cares for His universe, but in other areas of life as well. Look at your Bible, for example – a miracle, not only of inspiration but of preservation. Think about it. Look at the bread and wine, the next time you take Holy Communion – think about them. The bread and wine, those visible reminders of Christ's death, are designed to make us *think*. They call us to *remember*, and the more we consider them and think what they represent, the more our faith increases.

Don't just read the Bible or celebrate communion, baptism or any other sacrament of the Church without thinking about them. One thing is certain – we shall never come to believe more until we come to think more.

Danger!

5. In cultivating faith, take care that you don't become so preoccupied with it that you lose sight of God

I have met many Christians who become so engrossed with the subject of faith that they lose sight of the object of faith – God. Some have almost deified faith itself, believing that their faith can do all things, provide all things and be more than a match for all circumstances.

One thing that has become increasingly clear to me over the years is that faith, even natural faith, has such power that it can produce the most amazing results. Dr Ernest Holmes, in his book *Science of Mind,* says, "The idea that faith has only to do with our religious experience is a mistake. Faith is a faculty of the mind that finds its highest expression in religion ... but faith is an affirmative mental approach to reality."

If there is one thing that has been nagging at me as we have been continuing to meditate on this subject of faith, it is the thought that some may become so preoccupied with it that they will lose sight of God. There are signs that the Church is being influenced by the twin evils which are part and parcel of this twenty-first century – humanism and secularism – which put man at the centre of things and not God, so we must be careful that in upgrading faith we do not downgrade God.

"When we shift our faith from God to anything else," says Judson Cornwall, "we tend to think and exercise faith *for*, rather than faith *in*. Faith *for* makes us things-oriented, rather than God-oriented." We become more concerned about using God than letting Him use us.

Faith on an ego trip

6. Make sure your ego is exactly where it should be – at the feet of the Lord Jesus Christ

Why is this so important? Because if your ego is not fully surrendered to Christ, then you can easily use faith to embark upon an ego trip. I have no hesitation in saying that many Christians are caught in this trap, and are using their faith to boost their own ego rather than to bring glory to the Lord Jesus Christ. They would deny it, of course, but nevertheless, that is the way it is. If we have never come to the place which Paul reached when he said, "I have been crucified with Christ and I no longer live, but Christ lives in me" (Gal. 2:20), then we lay ourselves open to the misuse of faith.

One of the needs of our personalities, say the psychologists, is a need for power. We all have it, and we all try to make sure it is met – one way or the other. And nothing panders to our basic need for power more than faith. Faith produces within the personality a feeling and an awareness of power, and we can either use that power to meet our own ego needs or use it to honour and glorify the Lord.

One evangelist, a man known in many countries for his daring faith and his ability to produce the most astonishing miracles, told me in a moment of honest confession, "There is something within me that enjoys ordering God around ... that delights in being the focus of attention. Can you tell me what it is?" I responded to his honesty with equal candour and said, "Yes, you are using your faith partly to meet your ego needs, especially the need for power." He fell on his knees, confessed his failure to God, and rose to an even greater ministry than before.

A good idea – or God's idea?

7. Get as close as you can to God in prayer and through the reading of His Word, so that you are able to hear His specific directions for your life.

If we are lazy about cultivating our communion with Him, we are apt to get caught up in just good ideas, rather than God's ideas. 1 Kings 17:1 states that Elijah said there would be "neither dew nor rain ... *except at my word.*" Does this mean that Elijah thought up the idea on his own and then used his faith to bring it to pass? Was it a question of Elijah saying, "This is the way it is – because I say so"? No, of course not. In fact, right through the record of Elijah's life, we read this statement: "Then the word of the Lord came to Elijah." On Mount Carmel, when reviewing his past exploits, he says, quite categorically, "I have done all these things at your word" (1 Kings 18:36, NKJ). Elijah first heard from God before putting his faith into action.

This was also true in the life of Jesus. Take just one example – the man at the pool of Bethesda who was healed on the Sabbath day. Jesus, when challenged about healing on the Sabbath, said this: "The Son can do nothing by himself; he can do only what he sees his Father doing" (John 5:19). What is He saying here? He is saying that He looked up to heaven to see what God wanted Him to do – and then gave Himself to becoming the extension of God's will here on earth.

He saw what God was doing – and then did it with Him. If only we could follow this principle, it would deliver us from that most awful of maladies – presumption. Get close to God so that you know, not only the *logos* – His general will revealed in the Bible – but also the *rhema* – His specific word for *you.*

Stepping out

8. Act on the faith that you have and as surely as day follows night, faith will grow in you.

"Before you ask for more faith," says a well-known evangelist, "be sure you are putting to use the faith you already have." How good are you at practising the faith you already have? For example, when God clearly asks you to do something which you don't *feel* like doing – how do you respond? Do you take a step of faith and do it anyway? If you don't, how can you ask for more faith? When God asks you to make a sacrificial offering towards some special project – how do you respond? Do you say, "But I have needs of my own"? If so, how can you ask for more faith?

What happens if one day God doesn't seem as real to you as He normally does – how do you respond? Do you let your feelings dictate to you and refuse to pray or praise, or do you take a step of faith and say as David did: "Why are you downcast, O my soul? ... Put your hope in God, for I *will* yet praise him" (Psa. 42:5).

A great new adventure awaits you in the realm of faith, but you must act on what you already have. Jesus asked the man with the withered hand to stretch it out – the one thing he couldn't do. And yet as he responded with the grain of faith that he had, *in the process of obedience*, his hand was made whole (Mark 3:1–6).

As someone said, "Faith is like a muscle; the more it is exercised, the stronger it will get." Make up your mind that, from now on, you are going to get in some spiritual exercise. Find out what God wants you to do – and do it. As you launch out you will think you are stepping out into a void, but that void will turn to rock beneath your feet. You'll see!

Faith under test

9. Expect your faith to be toughened in the fires of testing

A look at how Jesus put the Canaanite woman's faith to the test in Matthew 15:21–28 will help you to face situations where your own faith is being tested.

Following a sharp clash with the Pharisees who were offended at His teachings, Jesus withdrew to the northern coastal area of Tyre and Sidon. As He was travelling through the country with His disciples, He was approached by a woman with a serious personal problem. Her daughter was possessed by an evil spirit, and so she pleaded with Christ for Him to deliver her. But here is the astonishing thing: "Jesus did not answer a word" (v.23).

How did she handle this apparent rejection and silence? She did not react with cynicism; no root of bitterness sprang forth; no hasty words were blurted out in retaliation. She responded by demonstrating that within her was the faith to persevere and persist. It was this, I think, that led Jesus to say of her, "O woman, *great* is your faith!" (v.28, RSV). What a compliment. No such honour was ever conferred by our Lord on any of the disciples! This Canaanite woman continued to have faith and hope despite the fact that there were no immediate results.

Are you the kind of person who *needs* to have answers and explanations for all the difficulties and problems God allows to overtake your life? If so, then God desires to bring you to the place where you can trust His love even though you cannot comprehend His purposes. And that, without doubt, is the highest level of Christian living.

Push ahead

Now we must gather up our thoughts in the form of a conclusion. One thing has become clear as we have pursued the subject of faith and that is this – faith is the principle by which we live and if we do not live by faith, then we just do not live – period!

It is not something that is optional, but something that is obligatory.

Many years ago, when my wife was alive, we visited the United States to enjoy a two-week holiday. While in New York we decided to visit an exhibition. To enter we had to drop a coin into a turnstile, which would then operate a release mechanism allowing people to go through.

A lady ahead of us dropped her coin into the slot and then stood back waiting for it to open. But it didn't, even though she had inserted the correct coin. The attendant said, "Now push against it" – which she did – and immediately she was through. It needed the slight, but aggressive "push" of faith, and when she gave it that – it opened.

It is a parable. Many have come into the Christian life, having paid the price of surrender, yet they remain standing at the turnstile waiting to go through. Now, having paid the price, you must literally press against the promises held out to you in God's Word, and walk through them into His wider purposes.

The text "... whatever you ask for in prayer, believe that you have received it, and it will be yours" (Mark 11:24), serves as a divine summary of all that we have been saying: "Whatever you ask for in prayer, believe that you have received it, and it will be yours." Notice, it says, "have received", not "will receive". Faith sees it as already done. The future is as big as the promises of God, and all that is needed to enter in is that slight, but aggressive push on the turnstile.

National Distributors

UK (and countries not listed below)
CWR, PO Box 230, Farnham, Surrey GU9 8EP.
Tel: (01252) 784710 Outside UK (44) 1252 784710

AUSTRALIA: CMC Australasia, PO Box 519, Belmont, Victoria 3216.
Tel: (03) 5241 3288

CANADA: CMC Distribution Ltd., PO Box 7000, Niagara on the Lake,
Ontario LoS 1JO.
Tel: (0800) 325 1297

GHANA: Challenge Enterprises of Ghana, PO Box 5723, Accra.
Tel: (021) 222437/223249 Fax: (021) 226227

HONG KONG: Cross Communications Ltd, 1/F, 562A Nathan Road,
Kowloon.
Tel: 2780 1188 Fax: 2770 6229

INDIA: Crystal Communications, 10-3–18/4/1, East Marredpally,
Secunderabad – 500 026.
Tel/Fax: (040) 7732801

KENYA: Keswick Bookshop, PO Box 10242, Nairobi.
Tel: (02) 331692/226047

MALAYSIA: Salvation Book Centre (M) Sdn Bhd, 23 Jalan SS 2/64,
47300 Petaling Jaya, Selangor.
Tel: (03) 78766411/78766797 Fax: (03) 78757066/78756360

NEW ZEALAND: CMC New Zealand Ltd, Private Bag, 17910 Green
Lane, Auckland.
Tel: (09) 5249393 Fax: (09) 5222137

NIGERIA: FBFM, Helen Baugh House, 96 St Finbarr's College Road, Akoka, Lagos.
Tel: (01) 7747429/4700218/825775/827264

PHILIPPINES: OMF Literature Inc, 776 Boni Avenue, Mandaluyong City.
Tel: (02) 531 2183 Fax: (02) 531 1960

REPUBLIC OF IRELAND: Scripture Union, 40 Talbot Street, Dublin 1.
Tel: (01) 8363764

SINGAPORE: Campus Crusade Asia Ltd, 315 Outram Road, 06–08 Tan Boon Liat Building, Singapore 169074.
Tel: (065) 222 3640

SOUTH AFRICA: Struik Christian Books, 80 MacKenzie Street, PO Box 1144, Cape Town 8000.
Tel: (021) 462 4360 Fax: (021) 461 3612

SRI LANKA: Christombu Books, 27 Hospital Street, Colombo 1.
Tel: (01) 433142/328909

TANZANIA: CLC Christian Book Centre, PO Box 1384, Mkwepu Street, Dar es Salaam.
Tel: (051) 2119439

UGANDA: New Day Bookshop, PO Box 2021, Kampala.
Tel: (041) 255377

ZIMBABWE: Word of Life Books, Shop 4, Memorial Building, 35 S Machel Avenue, Harare.
Tel: (04) 781305 Fax: (04) 774739

For e-mail addresses, visit the CWR web site: www.cwr.org.uk

The Discipleship Series

The *Discipleship Series* combines practical advice with biblical principles. Each dynamic title considers some of the most vital aspects of Christian living such as marriage, prayer and the Church. Essential reading!

- *9 Steps to a Renewed Life*

    Understand how God reveals His purpose and His plans. Learn to listen and obey and live life as God intended.

    ISBN: 1–85345–220–3

- *15 Keys to Enjoying the Presence of God*

    Discover how to increase, enhance and understand the sense of God's presence in your life.

    ISBN: 1–85345–210–6

■ £3.99 each

The Discipleship Series

The Discipleship Series

The Discipleship Series

■ *5 Insights to Discovering Your Place in the Body of Christ*

ISBN 1–85345–175–4

- Understanding the gifts in Scripture
- Discovering your ministry
- Developing your gift

■ *10 Principles for a Happy Marriage*

ISBN: 1–85345–173–8

- Engaging approach to marriage God's way
- Healthy marriage check list
- Practical advice and help

■ *15 Ways to a More Effective Prayer Life*

ISBN: 1–85345–174–6

- Revolutionise your prayer life
- Flexible suggestions for the individual
- Considers different personalities and lifestyles

■ £3.99 each

Available from Christian bookshops or by post from National Distributors

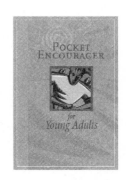

■ Pocket Encouragers

This new Pocket Encourager series offers biblical help, guidance and encouragement for everyone.

Each title explores various aspects of the Christian experience, such as relationships, Bible study and coping with responsibility. Great gifts!

■ Pocket Encourager for Men

ISBN: 1–85345–177–0

■ Pocket Encourager for Women

ISBN: 1–85345–178–9

■ Pocket Encourager for Young Adults

ISBN: 1–85345–180–0

■ Pocket Encourager for Leaders

ISBN: 1–85345–179–7

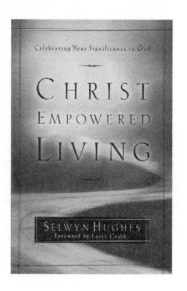

■ Christ Empowered Living

Christ Empowered Living sets out how Christ wants you to live as His follower and how He wants to develop your full spiritual potential. Selwyn delves into the human personality and shows how biblical insights will revolutionise your approach to the way you live and help renew your mind.

■ Chapters include:
- Who Am I?
- Why Do I Do What I Do?
- How Does Change Take Place?
- Monitoring Your Emotional Pulse

■ Hardback

ISBN: 0-8054-2450-4

"I believe God has been preparing Selwyn for many years, through hardships and joys, through speaking and silence, to write this book … It is a joy to commend this book to a worldwide audience."
Larry Crabb

"I always knew I had problems, but I never knew how to fix them. I finally learned how when I attended Christ Empowered Living."
Scott Hughes, attendee at Christ Empowered Living Seminar.